*The Penguin Modern P[...]
and diversity of conte[...]
together representative selections from the work of three poets
now writing, allowing the curious reader and the seasoned lover
of poetry to encounter the most exciting voices of our moment.*

MICHAEL ROBBINS was born in Kansas during the Nixon Administration. Some time later, he received his PhD in English from the University of Chicago. His debut poetry collection, *Alien vs. Predator*, was published in the US by Penguin in 2012; it was followed by *The Second Sex* in 2014. His poetry and criticism have appeared in *The New Yorker, Poetry, Harper's* and many other publications. He lives in America with the best cat in the world.

PATRICIA LOCKWOOD was born in Fort Wayne, Indiana, and raised in all the worst cities of the Midwest. Her poetry collections are *Balloon Pop Outlaw Black* (Octopus Books, 2012) and *Motherland Fatherland Homelandsexuals* (Penguin Books, USA, 2014). Her poems have appeared widely, including in *The New Yorker, London Review of Books, Tin House* and *Poetry*. In 2017, Penguin will publish her memoir *Priestdaddy* alongside a UK edition of *Motherland Fatherland Homelandsexuals*.

TIMOTHY THORNTON is a writer, composer, pianist and teacher, based in Brighton. His poetry and prose have appeared in numerous journals in print and online; his work for theatre and the stage has been performed at venues such as the Battersea Arts Centre and The Yard Theatre. His books of poetry include *Jocund Day* (Mountain Press, 2011), *Working Together for a Safer London* (Barque Press, 2015), *Water and Burning Effects On/Off* (Shit Valley, 2015) and *Broken Slat From Starling* (The Winter Olympics, 2015).

MODERN POETS 2

Controlled Explosions

Michael Robbins

Patricia Lockwood

Timothy Thornton

PENGUIN BOOKS

PENGUIN BOOKS

UK | USA | Canada | Ireland | Australia
India | New Zealand | South Africa

Penguin Books is part of the Penguin Random House group of companies
whose addresses can be found at global.penguinrandomhouse.com

 Penguin
Random House
UK

This collection first published 2016

001

Set in Warnock Pro 9.65/12.75 pt
Typeset by Jouve (UK), Milton Keynes
Printed in Great Britain by Clays Ltd, St Ives plc

A CIP catalogue record for this book is available from the British Library

ISBN: 978–0–141–98394–3

www.greenpenguin.co.uk

CONTENTS

MICHAEL ROBBINS

PATRICIA LOCKWOOD

TIMOTHY THORNTON

Michael Robbins

I Did This to My Vocabulary

The moon is my alibi. My tenders throw hissy fits.
My scalp's at the foot of the precipice.
My lume is spento, there's a creep in my cellar.
You can stand under my umbrella, Ella.

Who put pubic hair on my headphones?
Who put the ram in Ramallah?
I'm just sitting here spinning my spinning wheels –
where are the snow tires of tomorrow?

The llama is burning! My heart is an ovary!
Let's chase dawn's tail across state lines,
sing 'Crimson and Clover' over and overy,
till wonders are taken for road signs.

My fish, fast and loose, shoot fish in a kettle.
The boys like the girls who like heavy metal.
On Sabbath, on Slayer, on Maiden and Venom!
On Motörhead, Leppard, and Zeppelin, and Mayhem . . .

The Learn'd Astronomer

How long must we hymn the twinkling stars
before we admit they are no more distant
than the glow-in-the-dark stickers adorning
the ceiling of my first girlfriend's boudoir?

Teenage planet swimming into my ken!
Even then, I was so skillful a lover
that when I said 'Life is wasted on the living,'
the rivers ran for days with suicides.

Even then, I knew the stars to be empty cans.
There is the great Red Bull, watcher over
fevered gamers. To make me sixteen again –
I'd loose adders on the man who claimed such power.

No, you virgins, blessed in your ignorance,
for whom the night sky holds such romance,
the art of love is less mysterious than you suppose:
a plastic toy in a rubble of caramel corn.

These love poets couldn't write their way
out of a bag of kitty litter. The genitals, the heart,
the burning fantastical heavens themselves –
just junk in a Safeway cart I'm pushing
down to the recycling center.

Money Bin

I got a tattoo of God. You can't see it
but it's everywhere. If I seem out of it,
do the math. I was put on earth.
And then you were, making up your feet
as you went along. New thinspo clanks the spank
bank. New emoticon makes a Holocene.

If you want to get in shape you have to jog
your memory of Euclid. Jesus built
a ship in a ship shape and said
there's plenty of loaves in the sea.
Some Idaho you turned out to be.

Some money bin I, a rich duck, swim in!
The coins of you in my feathers like water
off my back. I count each red cent of you.
Now the rain with its funny money din.
The rain beats a tattoo of God any day.

Downward-Facing Dog

There is four helicopter running after person
and destroy his car. The truth, too, is fourfold:
1) life sucks; 2) for good reason;
3) you can sit under a tree;
4) the movie never ends, it goes on and on

and on and on. To write Nazi poetry
after Auschwitz is barbaric. And so inelegant.
What, you want to live with all those rodents?
Is *this* what you meant? Pay a little rodent rent?
The helicopter destroy four elephant.

Stand back! I am wearing pants! Same nun,
different ATV. God grant me the serenity
to rearrange your face. Grant me a GED.
If the killer whale's a killer, well,
you'd be one too in that whale's place.

Sea World is all that is the case.
Is that a crystal ball in your bosom?
I seem to see my future there.
Didn't your mama tell you it's impolite
to build in the empty house of the stare?

Dream Song 1864

Henry pitch his tone so low –
not on stars & sun –
on muskrat, sucker, frog & toad.
Who more low than that?
– Mr Bones: you like to know.
Triumphant Henry in palaver!

– who tho the ghost of Cotton Mather
his self wade ashore
'd talk of *facts* & objects
to show up phony all his blather, or
refute his taxing that & this.
So in Nature Henry is.

Henry commands loaves & fish,
dead upright – archaeologists
never more acute than he
when he fix his mind to furrow.
The doctrine of this hour
Henry mark. A cat most thorough.

Alien vs. Predator

Praise *this* world, Rilke says, the jerk.
We'd stay up all night. Every angel's
berserk. Hell, if you slit monkeys
for a living, you'd pray to me, too.
I'm not so forgiving. I'm rubber, you're glue.

That elk is such a dick. He's a space tree
making a ski and a little foam chiropractor.
I set the controls, I pioneer
the seeding of the ionosphere.
I translate the Bible into velociraptor.

In front of Best Buy, the Tibetans are released,
but where's the whale on stilts that we were promised?
I fight the comets, lick the moon,
pave its lonely streets.
The sandhill cranes make brains look easy.

I go by many names: Buju Banton,
Camel Light, *The New York Times*.
Point being, rickshaws in Scranton.
I have few legs. I sleep on meat.
I'd eat your bra – point being – in a heartbeat.

Reading Late Ashbery

I feel like a discarded Christmas tree.
Thanks for sharing. I can't hear myself think
about all this racket. As long
as we're discussing 'feelings,'
please turn to your information packets.

It took me twelve years to find this socket,
and if you think I'm throwing in the towel
just because my plugs have too many prongs . . .
I don't even *have* a towel. Oh, a *towel*.
No, I have a couple of those.

Far Candle

Sent to know of the silent wood,
tenants of earthfall, confiscation under
secular pretenses of [line broken off]
The tides which from afar candle,
crash toward [. . .] eliminate
class distinctions, I can, he said,
only dream of so many at one time,
the leafy shelter of the Skraelings.
It was for your sake the smoke the salt
surrendered spelled nothing at least
nothing this graphite hearth
[six lines missing] birth-days of dead kings.
So you will walk a mile in this polymath's
sand tonight, of which it is said
even the gods [have suffered] to learn the only
way to fall is down a rabbit hole or
[some other kind of hole,] or possibly
there is no burial in that northern ground.
The polestar is visible despite the lamps
of burning city-states, and we can steer
our drowsy boats into that fantastic harbor
[unintelligible] never to thatch huts again
[unknown number of pages used as fuel for cooking fires]
drinks cool spring water from an earthen jar.
And without it, at the solstice's dire genuflect,
we are as one who, composing a hymn,

Soft Pink Windows

Tried to use the spoon but
    the spoon shorted out.

Wants its robot raspberries back
    in the box of old receipts.

Bitsy Xanadus from the fever archive
    remix the minesweeper's tiny sex.

The religious left's turntablist
    threw T-shirts into the crowd.

Thus, you no-man-fathom,
    pee-shy, briar-brained, house-proud town mouse.

from **Karpos**

I glance at a twig, I take the twig to my bed, I tell it of manly love.
I tell my twig of the migratory song of the goose.
I tell it of the new form of companionship I propose in its name.
And now it seems to me I walked with my twig upon the
    brown earth
a thousand years ago, and a thousand thousand, before
    men were,
or women. It seems to me a twig might sup with the president
    of the United States,
and become president in its turn. And I will drop my twig in
    the gutter,
for I know other twigs in their hour will fall into my uncharted
    path forever.

And I have said I am a brother to twigs, and I say I belong to
    their nation,
and together we embrace the hay . . .

Secret Identities

POEM ENDING WITH A LINE FROM *FINAL CRISIS*

I hate – *hate* – the red sweater
and being called a cub reporter.
Stuck forever in a child's skin
while *he* gets Atlas' stamina.

I don't know where I go. A chasm
opens when I say –
well, you know. A wrong needs righting.
Two syllables. Then the lightning.

TUSK

Think of Mick and Stevie fighting
as the great white *Tusk* hove into view,
Lindsey rapt in his indicting
and in the cash and blow they blew.

Stevie Nicks, her nose on fire
like the hills above Malibu,
watches coyotes in fiery coats
trot down to drink from the fiery pool.

Self-Titled

'I used to be carried in the arms of cheerleaders.'
The National

Somehow I sidle, I kick-start,
I hot-wire my monkey heart.
I take my waking slow.
The president totes a vial of my cremains
and toots a vial of blow.
Nice president! I wish you'd just explode.

This is Uncle Tom to Ground Control.
I'm half awake. I'm a total fake.
The moon's the only natural object
visible from China's Great Wall.
The seasons rearrange themselves.
Winter, winter, Google, fall.

Fuck the moon. It's *pink*.
I was raised on Stax and Stones.
I pledged my troth to Mr. Bones.
The glaciers are melting
at a non-glacial pace. I have no
genes. I learn by going
out alone into America.

Fires, I've lost a few. Bee rustlers
infiltrate my privates. I just
died in my arms tonight,
brown cow. I'll walk into
sky-blue skeet shoots, baby blue.
It was nice of you
to. But you can put me down.

(2007)

Modern Love

My neighbor's whales keep me up at night.
They may not mean to, but they do.
I turn on Shark Week, plan a killing spree.
I'm all stocked up on Theraflu.

I love the word *chum*. By Kinko's early light,
the Korean children say *swim, swam, swum*.
I'm tangled in the jasmine of your mind.
I'm trying to heat the whole neighborhood.

Whoever has no house now, tough titty.
Whoever is alone will not hook up.
I already told you I think you're pretty.

Your refutation precedes you. I pawn
my iron lung. Whose whales these are
I'll never know. They lawyer up. I'm lying low.

Space Mountain

By the sweat of my grave, the dirt of my brow,
by the stage-diving douche bag, the nose-diving Dow,

by the suntanned sphincter and the jelly of roll,
by the mystery meat, by my bargain-priced soul,

by the whip and the fur in the black Cadillac,
by the winter storm warning and the eggs of the ox,

by the suit of hazmat and the muted ass-hat,
by what it's like to be, or beat on, the bat,

by the milk of the wolfman, by habitat loss,
by the beauty of black, by the red and white cross,

by the fiery furnace, by the frostiest fridge,
by Waco and Jonestown and by Ruby Ridge,

by the donkey with feathers, by dinosaur dung,
by the vaginal fang and the tar in my lung,

by missile defenses and difficult menses,
by tall and by grande, by mochas and ventis,

by the Egyptian dog, by the debonair moose,
by Natasha and Boris and squirrel on caboose,

by the panties that bunch, the knickers that twist,
by the device in my shoe that security missed,

by the saint in the well, by the lion who stank,
by the insignificant people I neglected to thank,

by the man on the street, by American thighs,
by the shit that I took that attracted no flies,

by the orbiting cobra, the comfortable lice,
by getting out of going through everything twice,

by getting out of going through everything twice,
by the saber-dicked tiger, the infinite mice,

by the cow in the moon and the mooncalf of gout,
by the bright boy who wants to know what it's about,

by the millionaire playboy's cape and his cowl,
by that wise old Zen master, the Tootsie Pop owl,

by the erasable duck, by the wascaly wabbit,
by licking the nun and by kicking her habit,

by the brain that I found in the girls' locker room,
by the horrible man-grapes of Fruit of the Loom,

by the bollocks I mind, by the virgin I'm like,
by the smell of teen spirit, the punch that I spike,

by hydro and chronic and eight-legged sparks,
by G-strings and tassels, by bummers and narcs,

by the temples I razed with a swish of my tail,
by the models of Jupiter I built to full scale,

I am a man of few words, each one a thrown switch.
Shall I name the mouth-breathers at whom I pitch

with superstitious loathing these excretions oozing bile?
Then pull up a chair. This could take a while.

To the Break of Dawn

I wandered lonely as Jay-Z
after the Fat Boys called it quits,
before the rapper from Mobb Deep
met up with the Alchemist.

I wandered lonely all along
The Watchtower's office front
in Dumbo, then across the bridge
that tempts the bedlamite to song.

From here you could've seen what planes
can do with luck and delta-v
as that fire-fangled morning
jingle-jangled helter-skelterly.

From *your gravity fails* to *whoops
there goes gravity*, from Céline
to Celan, from 'Turn the Beat Around'
to *And the Band Played On*,

from the *Live Free or Die*
of plates from New Hampshire
to Musidora vamping
her way through *Les Vampires*,

from *It Takes a Nation
of Millions to Hold Us Back*
to *Daydream Nation*,
from *Station to Station*,

I take this cadence from the spinning plates
where the DJ plots the needle's fall.
I take it, and I give it back again
to the dollar dollar bill and the yes yes y'all.

Live Rust

In the clearing I stand,
a boxer! Putting all your shit
in boxes, dragging the boxes
to this stupid clearing.

A man walks into his forties.
Says, *You lost me at 'hello.'*
I'm tying balloon animals.
Here you go. That's a rooster.

To burn out or to fade away?
I'm keeping my options open.
I'm looking for option C.
I'm boning up on Coptic.

I'm scrolling past the Dead Sea,
talking to Christ on the road
from Kiss My Ass to Damascus.
I kick my prick. I refute it THUS.

Be tawdry for me, thou.
Be like unto Sierra Mist
when it opens in the first
cold of spring. Be a Chippewa.

According to the oral history,
outside the Tastee Freez
you sucked on a chili dog
with your head between your knees.

The United States of Fuck You Too
is what you're about to receive.

You can shoot all the kids you like,
but you can never leave.

The mind is a terrible thing.
That outboard motor.
The tedium is the message.
The chimp signs *hugs* in his enclosure.

Is this Mick Jagger which I see before me?
Come, let me clutch thee.
I consider the lilies beneath me.
I tell the Magdalene not to touch me.

I tell the miniature schnauzer not to swarm.
I tell my willy it's getting warm.
I tell the content to fuck the form.

Sonnets to Edward Snowden

Who is the United States?
The grassy knoll elaborates.
Ask not what the Dew can do for you.
Ask about our special rates

for armed forces personnel.
All right, then, I'll go to hell.
These colors don't run –
red, white, and carbohydrate gel.

Navy SEALs are good to go
for *AvP* 2.0.
All along the White House fence

the Redskins mascot leads the chants.
Full fathom five Osama lies.
The blue-chip Dow industrials rise.

Who is the United States?
A snail paces by the Golden Gate's
anti-swan-dive hotline sign.
The snail is going to be fine.

Disabling a suicide
detector is prohibited.
A snail searches a starless sky
with the bionic arm he calls an eye.

The stars have got the bee disease.
The disappearing colonies
are no longer buzzworthy.

So ferry cross New Jersey.
I'm a black kid in a hoodie.
This land's the place I love. Et odi.

Who is the United States?
A grief ago – I'm bad with dates –
our fathers brought forth a queer
shoulder in a convex mirror.

I find it hard.
It was hard to found.
Unscrew the lids from the jars!
Prometheus outbound

on Aeroflot follows the Moskva
down to Gorky Park.
I'm proud to be a terrorist.

Mistakes were made at Plymouth Rock.
You might not be aware of this.
The ant's a centaur, more or less.

Günter Glieben Glauchen Glöben

Says here to burn the rich and take their shit.
I'm paraphrasing. I'm barely grazing
the surplus. Do the rich have inner lives,
like little lambs and Antigone?
They never give me their money.

Bill Gates, the great humanitarian,
stands upon a peak in Darien.
I said Bill, I believe this is killing me.
A sculptor sees the statue in the slab,
the shiv in the toothbrush. The stab.

I plump for Red October. Sink or swim
or wade or creep or fly or soak
it all in kerosene. Miguel Hernández,
tell me, if you know, why there's a darkness

on the edge of credit. My student loans?
Forget it. Burn it up. Let's go for broke.
Watch the shares go up in smoke. Nostalgia's
just another word that starts with *No*.

Peel Off the Scabs

Peel off the scabs! Unscrew
the daughters themselves from their jambs!
God became a man,
surely I can do the same.

I don't know wrong from light.
I can't tell my bright from left.
I really must be going.
I must be going soft.

I and I am I because I know
I wanna be your little dog.
Don't spit me out. Just swallow me.
I'll be your burning synagogue.

O Captain! my Tennille! the Eagles
will come and pull out his eyes.
Jesus coming back, they say,
and we'll all shout *Surprise!*

Is it any wonder I've got
too much blood on my hands? The calls
are coming from inside the house.
I'm sick of my insane demands.

To the Drone Vaguely Realizing Eastward

This is a poem for President Drone.
It was written by a camel.
Can I borrow your phone?
This is for President Mark Hamill.

Newtown sounds a red alert.
Mark Hamill asks if Ernie's burnt.
Every camel's a first-person shooter.
The Prez's fez is haute couture.

It seems strange that he should be offended.
The same orders are given by him.
Paging Pakistan and Yemen.
Calling all the drone-dead children.

The camel can't come to the phone.
This is for the drone-in-chief.
Mumbai used to be Bombay.
The bomb bay opens with a queef.

Not Fade Away

Half of the Beatles have fallen
and half are yet to fall.
Keith Moon has set. Hank Williams
hasn't answered yet.

Children sing for Alex Chilton.
Whitney Houston's left the Hilton.
Hendrix, Guru, Bonham, Janis.
They have a tendency to vanish.

Bolan, Bell, and Boon by car.
How I wonder where they are.
Hell is now Jeff Hanneman's.
Adam Yauch and three Ramones.

[This space held in reserve
for Zimmerman and Osterberg,
for Bruce and Neil and Keith,
that sere and yellow leaf.]

Johnny Cash and Waylon Jennings,
Stinson, Sterling, Otis Redding.
Johnny Thunders and Joe Strummer,
Ronnie Dio, Donna Summer.

Randy Rhoads and Kurt Cobain,
Patsy Cline and Ronnie Lane.
Poly Styrene, Teena Marie.
Timor mortis conturbat me.

Sunday Morning

Must you flush the toilet
while I'm in the shower?
That's a metaphor. It means:
one system, contrary aims.

Let us say that I have come
from beyond the Lyme fields
and ironworks of mortal men.
Would you flush the toilet then?

It's a yes or no question.
Sometimes I think you're in a coma
for there is no pupillary response
when I shine a penlight in your eyes.

Still speaking metaphorically.
We're all adults here,
except for the children.
We all have someplace we'd rather be.

Once, not many winters ago,
a man could record his favorite show
on magnetic tape in plastic casing
and enjoy it at his leisure.

Or so I imagine it,
living alone with the cat,
my amanuensis and all that.
Visitors tell her that she's fat.

Anthony comes around to play
'Burning Airlines Give You So Much More'

on my brand-new Yamaha.
I read him what I wrote that day.

I step from the capsule
out onto the surface of my apartment.
From here the earth looks like the set
of the Verizon Halftime Report.

I make the beast with no backs.
Someday a real rain will come
and wash all the scum
off my sheets.

I support the unborn child's right
to be spared the ghastly sight
of this briefly burning world,
this swiftly tilting dumpster.

All new speedways boogie
and misty mountains hop.
The telephone's been cut off,
I'm waiting for the clocks to stop.

If you love something, set it free –
that's stupid. Keep it close.
If I've killed one man,
I've killed most.

I'm having a feelings attack
out of the blue. Into the black
site, the multisided mudslide.
I'm just trying to find the bridge.

I Skype with Rose.
The heart knows what it knows.
Rose says, 'Go put a shirt on.'
All my friends are Scorpios.

I live alone with the cat.
It's been a long time.
Been a long lonely
lonely lonely lonely lonely time.

Country Music

God bless the midnight bus depot,
the busted guitar case.
God bless diazepam,
its dilatory grace.

God keep Carl Perkins warm
and Jesus Christ erase
my name from all the files in
the county's database.

The dog that bit my leg
the night I left the state,
Lord won't you let
his vaccines be up to date.

West Point to the south of me,
Memphis to the north.
In between is planted with
pinwheels for the Fourth.

Smokestack lightning, Jesus Christ –
whatever your name is –
bless my fingers on these strings,
I'll make us both famous.

How about that, the new moon,
same as it ever was.
You must've been high as a kite
when you created us.

So hurry, hurry, step right up,
there's something you should see.

The sun shines on the bus depot
like a coat of Creole pink.

God keep the world this clean and bright
and easy to believe in
and let me catch my bus all right,
and then we'll call it even.

Sweet Virginia

I got a letter from the government.
It said let there be night.
I went through your trash.
There was night, all right.
I consider how your light is spent.

I have butterflies a little bit.
I have some pills I take for it.
I've been up since four the day before.
Agony's a cinch to sham.

Don't worry about the environment.
Let it kill us if it can.
I give a tiny tinker's damn.
I put the ox before the cart.
Consume away my snowblind heart.

Fastened to a service animal
it is waiting for the beep.
It is waiting for the right to change.
Hello, I know you're there, pick up.

Out Here in the Fields

Out here in the fields
a technician dims the light.
Too soon to say for sure
if this coheres all right.

You ask what time the elephant
sat upon the fence.
Sounds to me like time to get
a few new elephants.

I dress up like a razor blade
and hide inside an orange.
Petition, little children, one
who finds you less annoying.

No orange can be compelled
to self-incriminate.
The jury will disregard
the thirty-seventh state.

Longshoremen and long shores,
short piers and ships in port.
Third planet from the sun, I'm told.
It won't stand up in court.

You got moxie, kid, mixing
ricin in the suburbs.
I'm gonna be a nicer person
and emulate the lovebirds

with night-lights in their hips
and UC Davis eyes.

We'll sing the *Mary Hartman* theme
until the great assize.

Anna Wintour's discontented.
I'm bathing in the nude.
I'm erring on the side.
I'm pretty sure we're screwed.

This is rocket science
in the Desert Father style.
Those weirdos in their caves –
man, you should read their file.

They made war upon their privates.
They had insects in their beards.
Once you got 'em talking,
they'd prattle on for years.

And I'd be more like them
if I were less like this,
a billion points of glitter
in a fathomless abyss.

Patricia Lockwood

from When We Move Away from Here, You'll See a Clean Square of Paper Where His Picture Hung

Eyebrows are his most expressive feature. He himself, straightened, is someone's eyebrow.

In moments of grave danger, his bicep turns transparent, and reveals a sizable ink-clot, with small rivers of ink streaming away from it to form his outline, day after day, year after year. This is to reassure his viewers, who continually fear his death.

'Popeye,' in his adolescence, goes through a period of floating off the page. His father sits him down and recommends an anchor tattoo.

Although he is 'drawn,' and although he is 'a place,' he is not a map. If anything, he is a 'cartouche': the area of a map that encloses information about the map itself.

He is often captured and sentenced to slave labor, always the same: to row oars in other moving words, and be whipped within an inch by ascenders and descenders.

Watching him works this way: he walks the length of your vision until he reaches the end. You gulp like a gangplank and he falls into the Drink.

Or: He disappears into the sunset, riding a little killie over and under the waves.

Or: His enormous boyfriend is named Perspective; he ties him to train tracks again and again.

Any piece of paper on which 'popeye' is printed counts as a Will, as it contains his signature, his witness, proof of his death, a list of all the property he owns, and the name of his inheritor.

Occasionally a schoolgirl will write 'popeye' over and over with a pink pen, and it is then that he wears a dress and pretends to be a lady.

Depending on the decade, draws seams up the backs of his legs.

Parts of his body exist only when he is looking at them. He uses his shoeshine to stare up his own skirt.

At the school dance, 'popeye' feels a pang in his belly and an urge to push. 'Why me?' he wonders. 'Why now?' Alone, he disappears through the door marked & and does what he must do.

When he is angry, a frizz of black ink appears above his head. No, forgive me. That is not ink at all. That is the least favorite hair of the typesetter, the one that emerges from the thought of his mother.

THE ONGOING CRIMES OF HIS MOTHER AND FATHER

His mother reaches out, hatches ink under him,
and commands him to stand and walk.

His father bursts into the room, screaming,
'What is the meaning? What is the meaning
of this?'

His mother rushes to explain, and feels
the pain of a strikethrough fly through her.

'Popeye' famously wets himself – the worst
mistake a young image can make.

His father lifts a ruler, brings it down hard
on his 'boy,' lifts a paint-stirrer up again.

The Salesmen Open their Trenchcoats, All Filled with Possible Names for the Watch

We wait in the house for just the word.
Dictionary salesmen line up outside the only door
in the world, and talk their way inside, and ask to see
the Mr., and ask to see the Mrs. 'Not here,' we say,
'never here.' The salesmen tighten their trenchcoats.
Their stomachs, we hear, are eating themselves.
A suggestion of something floats through the air
and hooks in the salesmen's nostrils, and tugs them
toward the table, where empty birds are waiting.
The salesmen open their mouths. Their teeth are all
black gaps, they sink them into the drumsticks. 'Now
music,' they command, and the piano becomes all
pressed-down spaces. Their briefcases are dictionaries.
The salesmen set them open, they gleam with rows
                              of what could own us,

and what will it be the salesmen ask.
We have not slept in weeks, waiting,
and somewhere in our faces, pouches
bulge with money to buy the eye, but
we stare and cannot choose, and then

we cannot choose 'stairs,' disaster: they thaw
and run like rivers, and salesmen bend down
to drink the snowmelt, and feel something
                     rise or fall inside them;

we cannot choose 'mathematician,'
and he climbs in the bath and cries
when displacement of water is less
than himself; and we cannot choose

'leopard,' disaster: an approximate cat
appears in our midst and gallops audibly
toward us, patterned all over with leper
      bells, crying, 'Get close to me,'

and the wind of his country is at his back,
but we cannot choose 'whoosh,' disaster:
and wind goes with a final gust,
      rush of a thousand doors swung-to,

and the dictionary salesmen slam themselves
shut but lacking our 'click' they cannot latch,
and their brass combinations swing free
      as they march away from us, and then

they are gone and we are glad. We lay ourselves
out in state and wait for them to come again: an hour
straight here and a solid month there lay bricks against
the bricks. Next year we will be ready. Next year we will
spend the money – if their green is the same as our green.
The oldest boy was next in line, but now at night our mother
opens her only book, trails a finger down the list of begats,
thinks how a small name continued, from head to hip
to toe, its babylineal descent, till finally it dropped
out of him. And his grass became our green. And now
at night we sleep on piles
      of endless independent means.

from The Cartoon's Mother Builds a House in Hammerspace

When she first landed here, she wandered for a while, living out of her own two pockets, until one day she came upon a square of lawn the size of a handkerchief. Below, from another world, the idea of a house was forcing itself upward, trying to come out on the other side clothed.

A chandelier already hanging in the middle of the sky.

The flowers all in clear vases.

A slot in the air for mail. Even a peephole. And a crack through which someone was saying, Who is it, what do you want?

One shop appears when she needs it: a model train store. It sells everything a town needs, from portable tunnels to instant road, but she lingers most over the miniature 'You Are Now Entering ____' signs. They have one for every city you can think of, piled together in a clear glass jar. She slips one in her pocket and lets it burn a hole there.

When she wants to travel, she sits on a bench in the middle of nowhere. The scenery train pulls out. The scenery train pulls in. When her ticket is right, she will leave on it, and ride to the end of the line.

She is always on the lookout for lines here; the line is her only natural predator. If she let it, a line would swallow her whole and then lick the corner of her lip, and lay in a black earthquake on her floor, and draw itself in black boxes all over her calendar. It would ride out to her yard and draw a tree full of grasshoppers until there was not a leaf left, and still not be full. The line says, 'When I draw a stomach around all of it, then I will have eaten.'

Her son keeps a line, she remembers, and feeds it a mouse once a month. As soon as the mouse is fully digested, it appears here in her house, a long tail snaking behind it.

Sometimes a line disguises himself, and goes house to house with a paper and pen asking for signatures. She refuses to answer. He raps, then knocks, then threatens to put a shoulder through her door.

She sends her son a book, with her pop-up house between the pages. He sets it aside and lets it gather dust. She raps, then knocks, then threatens to put her shoulder through the door, but still he does not open it.

She brought all her books with her, too many books. She makes bookends to hold rows of them together: geodes the size of her head, sawed exactly in half, all gray crystals on display.

The line would like to cut her up and hang her from the ceiling. If he did, you would see a clean white portal in each piece, like a hambone. She is tempted to let him do this – like all good cartoons, she believes in an Afterimage, where her colors will become their cool opposites. Where her hell-colored ham will become the blue sky.

The Church of the Open Crayon Box

Must be entered through the sharpener every Sunday,
else your name will be lovingly written in the Book
of the Down Arrow. The One Steeple to Every Church
                              rule breaks in half
in the Church of the Open Crayon Box; the One Bell
to Every Steeple rule breaks off its tip. 'Climb stairs
to the steeples,' the preacher commands, 'and let
every belltone ring out!' You can see the whole town
          from the steeple, and you exit the church through
            the view, and you walk through what calls itself

                              Flagpole – the town is a blot
                              on the town, but the railroad
is coming out this way and we must give them a smear
to see through the windows: now you pass the General Store,
that even your vaguest stick figure can enter, now you pass
a vacant lot: the post office isn't here yet, is only a set-aside space
in the center of the country's envelope; now you pass the voting-
place, where we stuff our handwriting through a slit. Tall trees
fall in the pinewoods, tall telegraph poles are raised, and words
inch along our wires: text text text stop, text text text stop.

And now you pass the Feed Store, which sells carrot and turnip
and sugar-beet tops – only the visible parts – and now Whitey
BaLavender's Hardware, where everything hangs off the hook
of its color, or color hangs off the hook of its all, where you work
your hands into cool washers, and work hands into nailheads
of the color blue, and watch Whitey BaLavender busy himself
          pouring crayons into bullet molds. You show him a list
          that says 'ax,' and he sells you a red line through it.
                    All up and down Main Street ponies are covered
                    with strokes as coarse as horse blankets. And once

you have drawn the ponies you begin to draw the saddle
shop, you grip the right color like a saddle horn and somehow
keep from falling off, and you ride to the edge of town,
where you draw the fur trading post, where they sell tails
of any shy animal, the rest of the animal gone down a hole,
where you trade in your skin for a possibles bag and wear
possibles bag where your skin was. Fat geese fly in any letter
you like but you need red meat for once, and write a splayed-
hide word like 'Deerslayer,' and take hold of the ending
                                        and drag it home,

and now you are almost there, now you are building the home
with hand-drawn Log Cabin Font, you are building it log
by log of course and smoothing the logs with a color called
Adze, you are biting the crayon to notch the logs and driving
in dots of nailheads. Stumps of umber surround you, and the sky
is beginning to look like sky. You are hoping a man can be really
        alone here;
                you are hoping your father can tell what it is;
and now only the doorknob is left to draw and in your enthusiasm
you shout at the paper, and the weather
                        changes just in time, not raining, beginning to spit.

from **The Quickening**

HE GROWS EARS, EYES, AND ARMS IN THE BELLY OF THE WHALE

I.

He grows ears, eyes, and arms in the belly of the whale;
he grows a way to be looked at; grows a broken nose
at the age of nine; grows an empty stomach, grows pieces
of pepper between the teeth; grows a third-grade education;
grows the Gettysburg Address; grows first the bones
of the hand, then grows recitation of the bones of the hand;
grows a pregnant teacher; grows the openness of jaws
at the local museum; grows his favorite text: 'Am I a sea,
or a whale, that thou settest a watch over me?' Grows
h-e-i-g-h-t-h in his spelling bee;

<blockquote>

then grows his grown up,
his gone to sea and grows
his own Gone Missing;

</blockquote>

HE BREAKS DOWN IN THE BELLY OF THE WHALE

II.

He washes the mouth of the whale; he swims toward
one unit of candlelight; he sleeps on a shipwreck inside
the whale and sends his smoke to the breathing roof;
he eats year-old bread in the belly of the whale
and the whale's hunger does not diminish, how?
he eats fat rudderfish in the belly of the whale and
the whale's hunger goes nowhere, how and how?
and slowly, he loses his way to be looked at; he grows
a way to be read at breakfast; he grows a Y and a fine
white spray;

> he grows his final words, 'Watch, the eye
> of the whale will swallow you also.'

The Arch

Of all living monuments has the fewest
facts attached to it, they slide right off
its surface, no Lincoln lap for them to sit
on and no horse to be astride. Here is what
                                    I know for sure:

Was a gift from one city to another. A city
cannot travel to another city, a city cannot visit
any city but itself, and in its sadness it gives
            away a great door in the air. Well
            a city cannot *except for Paris*, who puts
on a hat styled with pigeon wings and walks
through the streets of another city and will not
even see the sights, too full she is of the sights
already. And within her walk her women,
            and the women of Paris looking like
            they just walked through an Arch . . .

            Or am I mixing it up I think I am
with another famous female statue? Born
in its shadow and shook-foil hot the facts
slid off me also. I and the Arch we burned
to the touch. 'Don't touch that Arch a boy
we know got third-degree burns from touch-
            ing that Arch,' says my mother sitting
for her statue. She is metal on a hilltop and
so sad she's not a Cross. She was long ago
given to us by Ireland. What an underhand
            gift for an elsewhere to give, a door
that reminds you you can leave it. She raises
            her arm to brush my hair. Oh no female
armpit lovelier than the armpit of the Arch.

List of Cross-Dressing Soldiers

First there was Helen of Sparta, who did it only
with oil, no one knows how; then there was
Maggie of England, who even on the battlefield
put men back together; and then there was Rose
of the deepest South, who stood up in her father's
clothes and walked out of the house and herself.

Disguised women were always among them.
They badly wanted to wear blue, they badly
wanted to wear red, they wanted to blend
     with the woods or ground. Together
with men they were blown from their pronouns.
Their faces too were shot off which were then
free of their bodies. 'I never had any dolls I only
had soldiers. I played soldier from the minute
I was born. Dropped my voice down almost
into the earth, wore bandages where I didn't
need them, was finally discovered by the doctor,
          was finally discovered at the end.'

Someone thought long and hard how to best
make my brother blend into the sand. He came
back and he was heaped up himself like a dune,
he was twice the size of me, his sight glittered
deeper in the family head, he hid among himself,
and slid, and stormed, and looked the same
as the next one, and was hot and gold and some-
          where else.

My brother reached out his hand to me and said,
'They should not be over there. Women should not
be over there.' He said, 'I watched people burn

to death. They burned to death in front of me.'
A week later his red-haired friend killed himself.
And even his name was a boy's name: Andrew.

A friend writes to him, 'My dress blues are being
altered for a bloodstripe.' That's a beautiful line,
I can't help hearing. 'Kisses,' he writes to a friend.
His friend he writes back, 'Cuddles.' Bunch of girls,
bunch of girls. They write each other, 'Miss you,
brother.' Bunch of girls, bunch of girls. They passed
the hours with ticklefights. They grew their mustaches
together. They lost their hearts to local dogs,
                    what a bunch of girls.

I sent my brother nothing in the desert because
I was busy writing poems. Deciding one by one
where the breath commas went, or else it would
not stand and walk. This was going to be a poem
about release from the body. This was going
to be a poem about someone else, maybe even me.

My brother is alive because of a family capacity
for little hairs rising on the back of the neck.
The night the roadside bomb blew up, all three
sisters dreamed of him. There, I just felt it,
the family capacity. My brother is alive because
the family head sometimes hears a little voice.

I had been writing the poem before the boy died.
It then did not seem right to mention that burn means
different things in different bodies. I was going
to end the poem with a line about the grass. But
they were in the desert, and I was in the desert when
I thought about them, and no new ending appeared

to me. I was going to write, 'The hill that they died on
was often a woman, wearing the greatest uniform of war,
which is grass.' I know my little brother's head. The scalp
is almost green, where the hair is shortest. I know
my little brother's head, and that is where the ending
lives, the one that sends the poem home, and makes grass
stand up on the back of the neck, and fits so beautiful
　　　no one can breathe – the last words live
in the family head, and let them live in there a while.

The Feeling of Needing a Pen

Really, like a urine but even more gold,
I thought of that line and I felt it, even
between two legs I felt it, the legs I wrote
just now, a panic, a run-walk to the private
room with a picture of a woman
on the door, or else the line was long, too long,
I barged into the men's, and felt stares burning
hard like reading or noon, felt them looking
me up and over, felt them looking me over
and down, and all the while just holding their
pens,
they do it different oh no they don't,
they do it standing up, they do it at the window,
they do it so secret in a three-hour bath, they do it
aloud to someone else, their wife is catching
every word and every word is gold. What you eat
is in it, blackberries for breakfast are in it,
fat atoms of Shakespeare and Hitler are in it.
The sound of water makes me need to: Atlantic,
Pacific, Caspian, Black. I feel it so much because
I am pregnant, I am pregnant with a little self,
all of its self
is that spot on a dog that causes its leg to kick.
It kicked and I felt and I wrote that last line. Even
now it's happening. I eat only asparagus like arrows,
I am famous for my aim. I get almost none on my hands,
almost. Under my feet the streets, under the streets
the pipes. Inside the pipes a babble sound.

Factories Are Everywhere in Poetry Right Now

We are watching a crayon being made, we are children,
  we are watching the crayon become crayons
and more crayons and thinking how can there be enough
room in America to make what makes it up, we are thinking
all America is a factory by now, the head of it churning out
fake oranges, the hand of it churning out glass bottles,
  the heel of it churning out Lego men.

We are watching lifelike snakes get made, we are watching
lifelike rats get made, we are watching army men get made;
  a whole factory for magic wands, a whole factory
for endless scarves, a whole factory, America, for the making
of the doves, a whole factory, America,

  for the making of long-eared
rabbits and their love of deep dark holes. We are watching
a marble being made, how does the cat's eye get in the marble
and how does the sight get into that, how does the hand get
on it, how does the hand attach to the child, how does the child
attach to the dirt, and how does the dirt attach to its only name,

America. The name is manufactured here by rows of me in airless rooms. Sunlight is accidental, sunlight is runoff from the lightbulb factory, is ooze on the surface of all our rivers. Our abandoned factories make empty space and our largest factory produces distance and its endless conveyor produces miles. And people in the basement produce our underground. Hillbilly teeth are made here, but hillbilly teeth are made everywhere maybe. The factory that makes us is overseas, and meanwhile we, America, churn out China, France, Russia, Spain, and our glimpses of them from across the ocean. Above the factory billowing clouds can be seen for miles around. Long line of us never glances up from the long line of glimpses we're making, we could make those glimpses in the dark, our fingertips could see to do it, all the flashing fish in the Finger Lakes have extra-plus eyes in America. The last factory, which makes last lines, makes zippers for sudden reveals: a break in the trees opens ziiiip on a view, the last line opens ziiiip on enormous meaning.

Nessie Wants to Watch Herself Doing It

Doing what, I don't know, being alive. The green
of her is a scum on the surface, she would like
to look at herself. Should I have a memory?
she wonders. Of mother washing my frogskin
in muddy water? I do not have that memory.
My near-transparent frogskin? Mother washing
it with mud to keep it visible? I do not have that
memory, almost, almost. Warmblooded though
she knows for a fact, and spontaneously generated
from the sun on stone, and one hundred vertebrae in every
wave of the lake, as one hundred vertebrae in every wave
of her. All of her meat blue rare blue rare, a spot
on her neck that would drive her wild if anyone ever
touched it, and the tip of her tail ends with -ness and
-less. So far all she knows of the alphabet is signs
that say NO SWIMMING.

        So far all she knows is her whereabouts.
Has great HATRED for the parochial, does the liver
of the lake. Would like to go to universe . . . al . . . ity?

        She has heard there is a good one in Germany.
They stay up all night drinking some black sludge,
and grow long beards rather than look at themselves,
and do thought experiments like: if I am not
in Scotland, does Scotland even exist? What do I look
like when no one is looking? She would listen to them
just as hard as she could with the mud-sucking holes
in her head – and they, she thinks, would listen back,
with their ears so regularly described as seashell.
The half of her that is underwater would like to be
under a desk, the head of her that is underwater
would like to be fully immersed.

        I will be different there,

she thinks, with a powerful wake ahead of me.
When will the thinkers come for me. Visited only
here by believers. Is so deep-sea-sick of believers.
When will the thinkers come for me here, where
the green stretches out before me, and I am my own
front lawn. The green is a reflective green, a green
in the juicy shadows of leaves – a *bosky* even green –
a word I will learn to use, and use without self-
consciousness, when at last I go to Germany. I have
holed myself away here, sometimes I am not here
at all, and I feel like the nice clean hole in the leaf
                    and the magnifying glass above me.
She looks to the believers on the shore. A picture
                    it would last longer! shouts Nessie.
Does NOT believe photography can rise to the level
of art, no matter how much rain falls in it, as levels
of the lake they rose to art when Nessie dipped
her body in it. Nessie wants to watch herself doing
it. Doing what, I don't know, being alive. The lake
bought one Nessie and brought her home. She almost
died of loneliness until it gave her a mirror. The lake
could be a mirror, thinks Nessie. Would be perfectly
                    still if I weren't in it.

Revealing Nature Photographs

In a field where else you found a stack
of revealing nature photographs, of supernude nature
photographs, split beaver of course nature photographs,
photographs full of 70s bush, nature taking come
from every man for miles around, nature with come back
to me just dripping from her lips. The stack came
up to your eye, you saw: nature is big into bloodplay,
nature is into extreme age play, nature does wild interracial,
nature she wants you to pee in her mouth, nature
is dead and nature is sleeping and still nature is on all fours,
a horse it fucks nature to death up in Oregon, nature is hot
young amateur redheads, the foxes are all in their holes
for the night, nature is hot old used-up cougars, nature
makes gaping fake-agony faces, nature is consensual dad-
on-daughter, nature is completely obsessed with twins,
nature doing specialty and nature doing niche, exotic females
they line up to drip for you, nature getting paddled as hard
as you can paddle her, oh a whitewater rapid with her ass
in the air, high snowy tail on display just everywhere.
The pictures were so many they started to move. Let me
watch for the rest of my natural life, you said and sank down
in the field and breathed hard. Let me watch and watch
without her knowing, let me see her where she can't see me.
As long as she can't see me, I can breathe hard here forever.
See nature do untold animals sex, see nature's Sicko Teeen
Farm SexFeest, see her gush like the geyser at Yellowstone,
see the shocking act that got her banned in fifty-one states
including
Canada. See men for miles around give nature what she needs,
rivers and rivers and rivers of it. You exhale with perfect
happiness. Nature turned you down in high school.

Now you can come in her eye.

Why Haven't You Written

The past, when it was sick right down
to its roses, obsessively checked the mail.
We wore all of our pathways checking
the mail. We went into the woods because
we heard the letters rustling, and we swore
they sounded like letters to us. Even Thoreau,
on Walden Pond, checked his open mouth
every morning, foolishly believing it to be
the mail. We worshipped a great white
body that was an avalanche of good news,
and we slit it open in every part. 'That can't
go through the mail,' the postman gasped,
        'because that is a super-stabbed body!'
The super-stabbed body rose up, with many
butterknives sticking out of it, and said, 'I AM
                    the mail.' It had so many lovers.
Everyone alive had a finger in it, ripping it open,
sometimes with blood, deep bleeding wounds
of information all over the back-and-forth form.
It took a long time to be delivered then, and traveled
in sacks like shapes of women, and women were
full of secret sharp corners where their postcards
were poking out, and at last in their bedrooms they
sighed with relief as they shook out their sacks
with both hands, and faithfully and affectionately
and yours tumbled out, and even I am tumbled out.
Most letters were love letters until they were not.
That was when the mail began to change –
and 'enveloped,' the only word that was believed
to contain its meaning, was opened and found to be
empty. Back then it meant something when my letter
never arrived, and now after ten years reaches you,

who are dead or in love with a lookalike, or so full
of hate for me that you can barely see to read this.
If you're not reading this then it never got there,
        and both of us are married to someone else.
The body of the mail still waits for your knife.
        Why haven't you written. Why don't you write.

Rape Joke

The rape joke is that you were nineteen years old.

The rape joke is that he was your boyfriend.

The rape joke it wore a goatee. A goatee.

Imagine the rape joke looking in the mirror, perfectly reflecting back itself, and grooming itself to look more like a rape joke. 'Ahhhh,' it thinks. 'Yes. A *goatee*.'

No offense.

The rape joke is that he was seven years older. The rape joke is that you had known him for years, since you were too young to be interesting to him. You liked that use of the word *interesting*, as if you were a piece of knowledge that someone could be desperate to acquire, to assimilate, and to spit back out in different form through his goateed mouth.

Then suddenly you were older, but not very old at all.

The rape joke is that you had been drinking wine coolers. Wine coolers! Who drinks wine coolers? People who get raped, according to the rape joke.

The rape joke is he was a bouncer, and kept people out for a living.

Not you!

The rape joke is that he carried a knife, and would show it to you, and would turn it over and over in his hands as if it were a book.

He wasn't threatening you, you understood. He just really liked his knife.

The rape joke is he once almost murdered a dude by throwing him through a plate-glass window. The next day he told you and he was trembling, which you took as evidence of his sensitivity.

How can a piece of knowledge be stupid? But of course you were so stupid.

The rape joke is that sometimes he would tell you you were going on a date and then take you over to his best friend Peewee's house and make you watch wrestling while they all got high.

The rape joke is that his best friend was named Peewee.

OK, the rape joke is that he worshipped The Rock.

Like the dude was completely in love with The Rock. He thought it was so great what he could do with his eyebrow.

The rape joke is he called wrestling 'a soap opera for men.' Men love drama too, he assured you.

The rape joke is that his bookshelf was just a row of paperbacks about serial killers. You mistook this for an interest in history, and laboring under this misapprehension you once gave him a copy of Günter Grass's *My Century*, which he never even tried to read.

It gets funnier.

The rape joke is that he kept a diary. I wonder if he wrote about the rape in it.

The rape joke is that you read it once, and he talked about another girl. He called her Miss Geography, and said 'he didn't have those urges when he looked at her anymore,' not since he met you. Close call, Miss Geography!

The rape joke is that he was your father's high school student – your father taught World Religion. You helped him clean out his classroom at the end of the year, and he let you take home the most beat-up textbooks.

The rape joke is that he knew you when you were twelve years old. He once helped your family move two states over, and you drove from Cincinnati to St. Louis with him, all by yourselves, and he was kind to you, and you talked the whole way. He had chaw in his mouth the entire time, and you told him he was disgusting and he laughed, and spat the juice through his goatee into a Mountain Dew bottle.

The rape joke is that *come on*, you should have seen it coming. This rape joke is practically writing itself.

The rape joke is that you were facedown. The rape joke is you were wearing a pretty green necklace that your sister had made for you. Later you cut that necklace up. The mattress felt a specific way, and your mouth felt a specific way open against it, as if you were speaking, but you know you were not. As if your mouth were open ten years into the future, reciting a poem called Rape Joke.

The rape joke is that time is different, becomes more horrible and more habitable, and accommodates your need to go deeper into it.

Just like the body, which more than a concrete form is a capacity.

You know the body of time is *elastic*, can take almost anything you give it, and heals quickly.

The rape joke is that of course there was blood, which in human beings is so close to the surface.

The rape joke is you went home like nothing happened, and laughed about it the next day and the day after that, and when you told people you laughed, and that was the rape joke.

It was a year before you told your parents, because he was like a son to them. The rape joke is that when you told your father, he made the sign of the cross over you and said, 'I absolve you of your sins, in the name of the Father, and of the Son, and of the Holy Spirit,' which even in its total wrongheadedness, was so completely sweet.

The rape joke is that you were crazy for the next five years, and had to move cities, and had to move states, and whole days went down into the sinkhole of thinking about why it happened. Like you went to look at your backyard and suddenly it wasn't there, and you were looking down into the center of the earth, which played the same red event perpetually.

The rape joke is that after a while you weren't crazy anymore, but close call, Miss Geography.

The rape joke is that for the next five years all you did was write, and never about yourself, about anything else, about apples on the tree, about islands, dead poets and the worms that aerated them, and there was no warm body in what you wrote, it was elsewhere.

The rape joke is that this is finally artless. The rape joke is that you do not write artlessly.

The rape joke is if you write a poem called Rape Joke, you're asking for it to become the only thing people remember about you.

The rape joke is that you asked why he did it. The rape joke is he said he didn't know, like what else would a rape joke say? The rape joke said YOU were the one who was drunk, and the rape joke said you remembered it wrong, which made you laugh out loud for one long split-open second. The wine coolers weren't Bartles & Jaymes, but it would be funnier for the rape joke if they were. It was some pussy flavor, like Passionate Mango or Destroyed Strawberry, which you drank down without question and trustingly in the heart of Cincinnati, Ohio.

Can rape jokes be funny at all, is the question.

Can any part of the rape joke be funny. The part where it ends – haha, just kidding! Though you did dream of killing the rape joke for years, spilling all of its blood out, and telling it that way.

The rape joke cries out for the right to be told.

The rape joke is that this is just how it happened.

The rape joke is that the next day he gave you *Pet Sounds*. No really. *Pet Sounds*. He said he was sorry and then he gave you *Pet Sounds*. Come on, that's a little bit funny.

Admit it.

The Descent of the Dunk

First no one could dunk and then they all could.
The dunk evolved, and then stood upright, was even
perceived to be intelligent, with too big a brain
at the top of it, the ball. It grew upright and smooth-
skinned with a tendency toward religion, the dunk
stood up too fast, they said, and consequently has
headaches, and trouble breathing in spring when
it is so beautiful. The childhood of the dunk
               was no childhood at all.
He practiced on a paper route, throwing *The Sun*
to the same place each morning. Did not sleep long
but when he slept, the springs of his bed imparted
something to him. At night the streetlight floated
down and let him dribble it. Then there was school
there was every day school where he crumpled up
tests and tossed them in the trashcan. He shouted
TWO POINTS and had to stay after and copy out
the 'football' page of the dictionary, which could not
keep him down – he saw writers of the dictionary
at their desks, performing small silent neat dunks.
The crowd of the devoted watching. Like watching
is reading. Like it isn't. The dunk felt like a leather
study in space, and someone thinking *how* inside him,
and a perfected body in a leather chair wondering just
how high he can jump toward heaven. A leap sometimes
occurs within an animal, the dunk felt that happen
within him. He landed sure on his feet again and then
he was wholly himself. A joint so surely in its socket,
the whole city could go walking on it. All the rain
comes down at once in a single bounding drop,
and the wells of the countryside look up at once full,
and no open mouth is thirsty, and every mouth is open.

A great heavy body it weighed the dunk down. The dunk
and the moon pulled it up like the sea. The crowd of us
shouted his name to dunk him deep into himself. More
than half-moons in his fingertips, and rising through the air
in a loud round translation,
        and the air right then breathing him back.
Was the only complete thing in the world, was the dunk.
        Well that and everyone who watched it.
Goosebumps even on the ball. The ball spinning like
bodies could live on it, and whatever led up to the bodies
too. It stood up too fast, it got taller and taller, its women get
bellies like basketballs. A woman dunking! That'll be the day.
Yet here I am sailing over your heads, and then,
                with the sound, slamming into them.

The Hypno-Domme Speaks, and Speaks and Speaks

I was born as a woman, I talk you to death,
                              or else your ear off,
or else you to sleep. What do I have, all the time
in the world, and a voice that swings brass back
and forth, you can hear it, and a focal point where
my face should be. What do I have, I have absolute
power, and what I want is your money, your drool,
and your mind, and the sense of myself as a snake,
and a garter in the grass. Every bone in the snake
is the hipbone, every part of the snake is the hips.
The first sound I make is silence, then sssssshhh,
             the first word I say is listen. Sheepshearers
                    and accountants hypnotize the hardest,
and lookout sailors who watch the sea, and the boys
who cut and cut and cut and cut and cut the grass.
The writers who write page-turners, and the writers
who repeat themselves. The diamond-cutter kneels
down before me and asks me to hypnotize him, and
I glisten at him and glisten hard, and listen to me and
listen, I tell him. Count your age backward, I tell him.
Become aware of your breathing, and aware of mine
                    which will go on longer. Believe you
         are a baby till I tell you otherwise, then believe
you're a man till I tell you you're dirt. When a gunshot
rings out you'll lie down like you're dead. When you
         hear, 'He is breathing,' you'll stand up again.
The best dog of the language is Yes and protects you.
The best black-and-white dog of the language is Yes
and goes wherever you go, and you go where I say,
you go anywhere. Why do I do it is easy, I am working
my way through school. Give me the money
                    for Modernism, and give me the money

for what comes next. When you wake to the fact that you have a body, you will wake to the fact that not for long. When you wake you will come when you read the word hard, or hard to understand me, or impenetrable poetry. When you put down the book you will come when you hear the words put down the book,

you will come when you hear.

Timothy Thornton

from 3 Lute Songs

(BONE, BREVITY)

As arched out sunning
dogs we guard the scree, we heard the river
mark a syllable so nearly

undeliberate under stars
as to be our choice value, we
heard our voice change.

There was untenably the whole
situation, but I knew we had been paddling,
or simply less than needing to.

In a room of glassy air I know
you were away until I could not know
the room. I have not made

you hear me hurting in the glass,
I will not swim again.

and something is flowing through you, from your head downward through your neck and chest and out arm by arm, finger by finger, then further down your trunk, and leg by leg, toe by toe, and so on; not so much a kind of golden light, or anything which might osmose from an angel wrapping his luminous, muscular wings around you, but a more ineffable humour, perhaps the marrow of that half-attentive black crow which, you remember, prevented you, by standing on your neck with its claws tugging at the skin above your veins, from sitting up or moving when you found yourself supine on the back seats of that dusty empty airless bus for days on end through some desert, wondering for long parched hours how the previously inert fungus you had been watching in your bedroom for weeks was suddenly able to extend in thin foot-long rods or wands out of the coffee mugs, meeting and joining each other in intricate hexagonal patterns, each such union marked by one tiny, sticky, glistening, bright red orb of spores, and wondering how thousands of the local children had by the evening of your departure come to be playing in the park with replicas of these rods or wands of fungus, and why the only way to win in the game these children were playing with these wands was to return after the distraction of a dropped ice cream to find that you had been eaten by a ghost in pacman, and worrying that the marrow of this crow is not, honestly, fluid enough to flow through you at all without instead inducing in every one of the thousand neighbourhood children a brief hallucination, like those splintered out from a dream, of a closed and unlit universe entirely of vaults, a perpetual catacomb, cyclical and unvaried, deep in the marrow of a wingless, beakless crow, the final and blueprint crow, formed only of a single unsegmented bone, the shape of a torus, covered in black feathers which glistening and sticky way out there on the outer surface meet and join and flow through each other –

PESTREGIMENT

Dann wurde ich mit den nicht übereinstimmenden Tönen
　der menschlichen Stimmen dort geschlagen,
die mir wie den wilden Gänsen schienen, die in der Luft gackern;
Und der Fluss Themse ist ein schönster Anblick,
Zu die Dampfer sehen, nach ihm bis zum Tag und bis zum
　Nacht zu segeln.

They ah, well now you, the whispered you, that wait
that they would well, that even they would hold you
to it you, better hushed, clock:

                              the still at wheel in
brittle silhouette, the chapel shell a powerhouse
disguised, where were these lawns let daub. Argyll
wirework stacks-concentric you without this in-
stallation you, without howl to abate now. Their piss
worm lens O you mendacious little god explain this
hangman out, committee blanket out un-elect you, un-
notice arm-hair breeze deny mycelium your sentiment.

Stress capacity over the fuck of trigger cadence this can't
happen. This can't happen. A chlorine happy ploughman
sinuses to dusty them black scattered in relief, they wink
addenda tick one grit rings boys' eyes pink. Okay prison
songs plastered-orbital past you obviously

                              enough say it
to your face while they obviously can. Cordon remember-
you gathers-home no sweet-briar, no bonfire. Dog fortune
torn off a cheek now sense danger stops you, singing the
pretty-pretty wasp moral, any idea how brave marks it
for now airborne, now call it happened because it did.

You'd look up at the flags at wheel, something look is
not right, on the entrance of Southwark Cathedral. Grey
squirrels are not everywhere and the tea tab will not pull
properly or easefully back. The sheer of it look at that look
at that you, the better hushed, jar that they would tock and
buzzing in the matchbox kick and bellow the whispered ex-
pect ganglion ah damaged parity in the dossier, your new
fatt'ning
       lip clean bitten through is merely colder merely
on-camera consolation roster hum, something else say
researchers altogether. Pigtail itinerary warms down you.

Your Albion slack having eaten mandrakes under brute
encouragement pales slacker. Settlement only eyot aerial
just drive you, filamentous outgrowth of a bitch, escaped
their dead-mesh sifting. Clock: that sounds like something
you should definitely never do. Kids wave out the Volvo
to the pyres and a dog. They hangman-posit they, they uh
lawns just perform said anything about Shropshire just
three-point the hell to grips with this software now only
drive, alchemy
       this, into fucking in the grit, which is tock
as it is felt, it'll do you hey riven at the cirrus broadcasts.

Braying recoil they kindle terse you, dumb you, tock
suspended, sky only a jolt cubicle away. In all directions
valent news you tock and sway predictable you fucking
auroch in your velvet glove. Tock

of a gas mask tock. Tock
like you're on a roll imagine jasmine on the motorway, un-
vector blame mightn't they. In both directions procedure
the border standard which means it is safe in, or out, to
flatland you, ha

flood-lit ha well, they did stoke this you
sorry eyeless. Limp in to your pink kids. Late-caressing
visors is ideally hoar frost, is lever, they echo down to bed.

Up shepherds. Mornings the bum shaman gets you, uh
the whispered dank to your allotment in

turn. Aitch
sounds living proof over leaves. There are benefits, look
at others look, alike in polycarbonate. Until exchanges
clog they might just strip until you matt chest hair you
sick down

beat they low breath curfew at you in sweat-
haunt violence thinking, of biting. Sniff through it reap
and hard, tensile facing irrelevantly North-East tock, daub
the place. Semen curl surplus there hey

are benefits, look
at exposed roots now and chilling you, now never learn.

NEVER un-shell flagstone calf-pink for the sake of the
sake of taking it on
                    the taking it 'on
the chin', look up learning-in-play for the
trip, men strip
                    men, you ha must keep the masks this you
, uh granite
shoulder dog a
                    pocketful of 'you are enjoying
this too much sir'. Cannot we've a bit less unavoidab-

ly cerebralgic whinnyings in the casings boys, the sun
homing in over slow setback mills and those

thighs you graueþ in
                    grene to noht and fuck-vault
complete for now airborne because it happened.

Well now. You the well the stuck, hush
now in the sanctuary oscill ha trunk-dialling the
    ha shit poultice-guy there's no (1) SWEET-
                    BRIAR, no (2) BON-
    FIRE, no (3) STRAWBERRY-WIRE, no
(4) CO-LUM-BINE. And can the
                    physician and can
                    the physician and
                    can the physician and can

this transaction some last-ditch be for whatever to heed.
Chipper-head head above the booted flood-lads, lads, O
tact-god might have happened it at sea. NEVER let them

hear you, dumb you, relief you talk that brittling-up. No
sweet-bullshit eh no flood-lighting. Definitely something
you should definitely never do. Flick it over in your mouth

trigger easing-tock for masked him and you-collateral.
NEVER clock the ill at ease at wheel. There's a lawn let
seed. There's a squirrel. It's very still. There it goes boys.

NEVER you, the whispered slant you this unsure
                                    of plague-
regime you,
                you, your kids giggling at the silly-walking
                                        spores.
NEVER attend-to a glass against the skep-wall pressed:

ah, they ah, shrill-hanged, corroding nan-music amongst
other well, measures (

                        you see if you can't

                            hear the sweet wicks

                        frosting pylon noise not

                            a field away to get it

                        took, get it out) you Smith

                            uh cavity icon *Smith*

                        will lastly disconnec-

                            t your cisterns as

                        movingly as   Sunday-soon

By the gable you, scrip-tattered polythene gust bloodying a
skin trellis. Yelping is funny and refers to upright vessels

they meted O watching you sick it onto the kerb, wholly,
every single word an equal and opposite so try it: at last

recursively hello empty room behind everything. Recon-
figure ports as ears mightn't they and mend everything,

the committee by the skies breezes you, silencer of orchards
and pester capsule hum and kick and warn O ribboned what

you've done to you. Each thing is as un-right. Properly silent
no traffic peals at you dogs

your kith. Greet little airy
                          pockmarks on the carriageway

with absolute loss aptly. Hey
                          blinking on the tarmac we now
let's really bank on movement, and tock and you, tired tock.

from Jocund Day

HART'S TONGUE

In the mortice my tattoo of (in an
urn) your skin, strenuously on
        your face which

mortice / I would be O ungentle
at in falconry and tattoo forecast,
        keep this: close:

your held skin (in an urn) to mortice
your: ah hairline reveille, keep this:
        safe: outside: now

covert now blinding. Presentiment, now
below these our gulls of: sand catenary: your
        face that is most culled,

now I've got some piss and lager and some
theft there on your chest adjutant birdsong isn't,
        strenuously

        together here amassed:

        amock: male. We can tell this from
            our backs, I tell it from yours, repeatingly
        to mortice (in the

barrow where the pins fall and stones
are tumbled effortlessly to a sheen) us,
        or just to brush up, once
        enough against you

from Trails 01/07/2011

/

it is riot makes me a limited
  man horny flung against
a wall this shatters to know
  nobody else is missing
a thing stopped at the kerb

still spinning. Still there we
  are inhaling sodium flare
each other and the summer.
  I forget everything cleanly as
a treat apart from water.

Bell fundamentals, ah water
  flow me down *The Strand*
rename every shop *Alain*
  de Botton or *Alain 'de'*
de Botton see if you can't

further dement the burlesque,
  be the world's leading away
from home skin care system
  company. *Nigel Pargetter*
has almost landed. An air

thick in violence beautiful un-
  lyric failing to trick deployed
love into grained suture stank
  the sex flight as it clocked us
and / was away. Apart from sirens

water rung siren bells sodium
  flare I've been coming, almost
for five months now *Professor Brian Cox* why
  are you here licking

  the leather on your crutches
water is fundamental. I mean

  sirens our water-gong bell our
crutches are
  listen,

Constable B—— is gorgeous
  state apparatus. If he sang
to me I would get a piss/grit tattoo of
  the heat death of the ringroad
and never stop wanking

10.xii.2010

now stop the injured bird's heart. Our hero
ejaculates just as the hat-pin pierces the rat's
heart; the cop's heart is felt in the ears and
in the temples; abrasive crepe pulse, anechoic
linen, rolling his stark winter sky right out
into the bedroom and around the city's heart,
lapping at the street-lamps as it goes:

if you see a tendon or a nerve, it
should be a heart-string, make it one, make
sure to lash it to the sky, which is as much
hate for the riot helmet as it is love for
no riot shields. Can someone please put some
towels down for the horses now, they're
getting iron dust all over the tarmac, said

the street, and little bits of tarmac on their shoes.
Something like a clock strikes. 'If there are no towels
use newspaper.' Find out the badge number tenderly, by
massaging the prostate, and stop that injured
bird's heart (your hands might shake) by applying
gentle pressure (just enough to stop the beating) between
you and me (and the thumb and forefinger)

Broadcast

  In newer gull whip again weeping, sitting
on a bank I broke myself at neck
  to music wrack unspoke or hewn
undeeply, partsong tête à claques

sheet glass
ground in floor

  pressure evidence undubious
such burdensome extortion as
  borne in looking mind how tired
we are with two takeaway teas

  we just hugged, sat on a high up bench
  somewhere not that secret really
off the Lewes Road, afternoon of gold
and magpies on a cusp. But no wholly

  depth-charge branch is too white, padded
shot a mushroom cap a cheapened rink
  ice age glass of frozen, uplit tongues
unleaven how I never meant for you to drink

  a glass of day-old wholly sincere
spit who under maketh spring sew
  tongues into my pocket tongue
of day-old really salt-sincere snow

bell ring
lhude sing
  and not just sitting on a bench
how much we want to fuck in circling spring

the edible dormouse in my teeth lets slip
its tail fur; the crossbill digs into the warm
   pinecones of me, shine a torch
through my wiry fingers til the loam

mud and shit give
mere as brim immobilized
watching magpie tower
relay but

   on a high street full subduing beyond
what hurt dare not be again at stake, back
   for instance in a fall or lover, O lord
break on a bank or bench my neck

it was in the second half of the nineteenth century, during an otherwise familiar and unremarkable dream about maps of dreams, that a new and worrying map, with some very unusual properties, was discovered: it was a map of a dream about maps of dreams, itself of course featuring locations which represented dreams, within the dream represented on the map, about maps of dreams; these little glitches brought to bear on the top-level dream texture those threats, either of a diminishing recursiveness, or of a sudden erosion or porosity in an otherwise familiar and unremarkable concentricity of realities, which can lead in the worst cases to waking up confused and frightened; they were improperly marked on the map because no adequate symbol had yet been discovered, and it was for exactly this purpose that the courtesan, when she awoke from the dream, devised the moth – still, to this day, the marker of a sinkhole between realities, which can lead if mishandled to the creation of inward-plunging dream-worlds never to be escaped from, or, in the worst cases, to waking up confused and frightened, having thought that you had already done so –

Footnote: Not every head is Anthony Head's head. While it is true that Anthony Head's head is Anthony Head's head and therefore is without doubt *an Anthony-Head's-head*, supposing the possibility of other *Anthony-Head's-heads* which somehow do not belong to Anthony Head, each would still also and individually be an *Anthony-Head's-head*. Now, Anthony Head's head is so definitely an *Anthony-Head's-head* that calling it Anthony Head's head is quite sufficient, rather than the more accurate Anthony Head's *Anthony-Head's-head*, because Anthony Head's head and Anthony Head's *Anthony-Head's-head* are precisely the same thing, *i.e.*, Anthony Head's head. It will be obvious to the attentive reader that were Anthony Head to become the headmaster of a school, Anthony Head's *Anthony-Head's-head* (*i.e.*, Anthony Head's head) would more accurately be Anthony Head (Head)'s *Anthony-Head-(Head)'s-head* (*i.e.*, Anthony Head (Head)'s head), but this scenario would perhaps be more than many could take; certainly, it would do my head in, and it would probably do Anthony Head (Head)'s head in too, his Anthony Head (Head)'s *Anthony-Head-(Head)'s-head* (*i.e.*, Anthony Head (Head)'s head); and most likely he, Anthony Head (Head), would head up the stairs to his office to have a word with himself, clear the whole thing up with a head-to-head, or, more accurately, an Anthony Head (Head)'s *Anthony-Head-(Head)'s-head* (*i.e.*, Anthony Head (Head)'s head)-to-Anthony Head (Head)'s *Anthony-Head-(Head)'s-head* (*i.e.*, Anthony Head (Head)'s head). This head-to-head (more accurately, this Anthony Head (Head)'s *Anthony-Head-(Head)'s-head* (*i.e.*, Anthony Head (Head)'s head)-to-Anthony Head (Head)'s *Anthony-Head-(Head)'s-head* (*i.e.*, Anthony Head (Head)'s head)) would of course be going on entirely in Anthony Head (Head)'s *Anthony-Head-(Head)'s-head* (*i.e.*, Anthony Head (Head)'s head) [*Fig 1*]

Superhero Detective Novel

In the petrol station window Pepper's ghost
sticks his chewing gum to an architecture of
how this makes you feel, therapeutically an airport
shaped like the air in an oboe snakes

round your fuselage like bus routes that don't
suit you take them off / a massive petrol station
made of horseshoes and expensive water,
Pepper's ghost stares himself out of the frame.

Impossibly planes land at the petrol station
and claiming the land for life and food, they arrest
get out down sliding corrugated metal affixed
with chewing gum. Look at yourself in the framed

mirror. Some serifs you have there. Those bus routes
really don't suit you. Take them off. How you
being a series of cantilevered brass frames ever
manage to eat food I'll never leave too close to the reactor.

What you need is forty computers. Captain Computer
arrives. She says, Take them off. Get out. Captain Computer
claiming the land for forty computers shouts GET
OUT. This is seriously hard work. Too close

to the reactor fifteen horses, as usual: BAM KAPOW
feverfew set oxalis nightjar to a hell-fled motorway unit
fat for threat haste in a sky that's been backlit in blood
SIT DOWN it wants printing it wants BAM KAPOW FUCK

LAND in a city diagonal every ghost LIFE is a petrol station
computer captain you know FOOD are you chevrons are

you a traffic diversion unreasoning ridge in a circular
bus route, GET OUT. I'm going to a fancy dress party

as how this makes you feel / everyone needs a superpower
and flat back in a brassy grille one thousand starlings
trying to rhyme with each other drape the bus routes back
over your shoulders and leave you stood there, the only

petrol station unhaunted. Everyone needs a superpower,
as vessels snake interstitial into an organ that floods
the distance between you and sky. The petrol station
closes as you approach. You walk away and it opens.

The cafe as you approach sets the sign to closed.
As you withdraw they set it again to open.
The petrol station closes as you approach.
It re-opens as you withdraw. The cafe closes

as you approach. It re-opens as you withdraw.
Everyone needs a superpower. This is yours.
You hollow out every factitious object or thing,
reality closed down to an intractable pair

of alternatives, all there is. Your superhero name is
Captain Reality Closed Down To An Intractable
Pair Of Alternatives, All There Is. Life forever
walking between a petrol station and a cafe.

You are the reactor somebody else will one day
stand too close to. Think about how this makes
you feel. In your reflection starlings peck
at bus routes between things. It suits you. Take them off
                                                    and get out.

Horoscopes

1.
A billygoat tried on a litre of positive narratives
splosh! and unfurled for a dime a cartoon limb in hemmed
slapstick, not just for the denouement a pierced succulent
but evermore and sluice: a too-shallow tray its dehydrator.

2.
That a cactus burst in brackets by any other cosmology
is a mean-spirited transmission from banned piercability,
labile and flapping in the quadrant, tell your children,
through whom the blind threat is slotted like a crossed orbit.

3.
Your emollient wolves provide references, the moon is
proportional and locked out, you are in the darkroom,
the vuvuzela is exemplary, an ignited Olbas fountaineer weeping
melts, and you should work harder at your job, say friends.

4.
A planetary backspace fucks you up because it grinds
the orrery's gears, and your life was always fucking pinched
anyway. You are limited and unreasonable, say friends.
Something less limited, more unreasonable, billows at you
                                                    terribly.

5.
But often what is terrible retreats as if diagonally. Rainfall
too may be allowed to fail on a mechanical donkey because it is
a certain height, and there are other reasons too. On the pier
the shithead gulls will try to share your food like flying shire
                                                    horses.

Silo Sonnet for Greasy Receivers

There is a clatter in the way they use
the tracks, the jackal says, parable eyes
as if he thinks that peristaltic ease
he would detect snaked over camel-backs weighs
heavy in its absence on pistons whose
first instinct is just to cauterize
a gradual climb or gradual decrease
into a sort of platform that can raise
or lower, nothing else, which just accrues
rust. The jackal looks at you and sighs,
leaves the creaking steppes, leaves you in peace;
your eyes peel open, noting through the haze
you don't even have four dromedaries.
You've a headache and some annoying news.

Sonnet

for Richard Dodwell

Planes flatten over. Just in case, let's cast
stretches of absent wire in the sky;
leave no canisters empty; scatter, tasked,
some candle freight whose corrugated iron
cells bear codes plunged off to away archives
of those darkened tygers cast in wax,
wick, camphor-wood, spread out as airless doves,
their transit euphemised, deployed collapse.
There is a special grey, the sky can host it,
set along an unreal shelf for missing
information, life stuff, always outlasted,
like most things unreal, special, missing.
The point of flattened skies is things are missing.
Like other things, flattened skies go missing.*

---

* Dear Richard, I'm just off the plane at Gatwick, and am on the train
now to Brighton, but seen from the plane window what must be called
the clouds are in what must be relative close-up still seeming distinct
only in what must nevertheless be their immense distance from you and
are by the look of them implausibly, unreasonably still, they hang like
something deeply familiar whose capacity for change or persistence
through time has suddenly been amputated, unscalable terrains in every
aspect a simulation of suspense, they are total and between and are a sec-
tion, they are ideal and romantic, a blueprint of what you could rolling
out to the horizons expand and see should you having cracked a single
moment open and into it poured an infinity felt yourself too fall in and
brighten through in sympathy, the layers stretch as far as they can and
slightly more gold, and perhaps in each of these individual ecstatic
interims, in each infinity of vapour cliffs and vapour islands hanging
screened off from sun and land between snowblinding layers, perhaps
with each one of these newly-minted images of a world, every ended soul,
from a sparrow to a god, is billowing by billowing and frond by frond
memorialized, but it seems less than likely

Christmas Voicemail for the Loneliest Whale in the World

if you can hear
beneath this flatline, think
for me coldly of a number station rotating
keen as a massless blip in the air
above an allotment seen from a train;
buildings became covered in unfamiliar area codes
and let us reverse engineer for you the process
by which tatty polythene itself became more
everywhere than your kind. If you can hear beneath this
                                            hum, you
are the location of hurt-ready trust in
about to arrive or recently went or facing at going:
some familiar loop of banishment then return, fizzing
out in an orbit whose true condition is distance, and being
on the other side of what you can hear,
if you can hear it, and whether you ever wanted to.
Nobody's teamless stripe in the seabed gathers for you
a funicular schedule of nearly
detecting company
twice per universe, regardless
and wanting audition. In a parallel whale,
if you can hear this exists
not an averaging out, but the
cumulative total pulse of what is redundant
in this, our heartwarming coldly entropic hiss
of misremembered antennae, company.
For christmas I've got you a bottle
of nice whisky and a phone charger, if you can hear this

of what must be a limitless number of coincidences in timing whose nature comes after the fact to seem quite cavernous, we shall for the present purpose refer specifically to that which occurs when you are half sleeping, in bed with a wholly sleeping lover, and have allowed your hearing to settle and slow to the rhythm of their breathing, acutely aware of any increase in intensity, any approach toward that tiniest excess of pressure which would tip the breathing over some quite physical threshold or cliff and render it a snoring, when suddenly after a silent pause or trough a new inhalation seems to continue, and continue and continue and continue, until it has become something completely new, and you realise that in some intricated and very personal concomitance of timing, just for you, the calm intake of breath to which you are the only auditor has become a bracing traffic roar, the car outside already gone away as quickly as you could figure its identity, and your ears, deaf to parallax because of pillows and such keen attention to the rhythms of your oblivious lover, have confused the breath and the roar, before the passing car was close enough for breath and roar to be distinct in any case; and then there are the gaps which appear, the tearings-apart which happen in the last two seconds of your memory, between the car and your lover, and the breath, and the noise, and the point at which the breath had become so loud and violent that the elastic of your believing in it as a breath was snapped, and some other understanding had then to fall into place, and the inside of your lover's chest opening up to take in more and more and more air as the breath became as vast as it could possibly become before the elastic of your believing in it as a breath was snapped; and all these instances, the world prying back by just a touch into your memory and in a funk of dilatory yawns opening up to you the wideness of the night, all these pullings-apart are much the stranger for their being the result of two things happening so precisely together and at the same time –

from Trails 01/07/2011

irradiate kerb curtailment. Burning utmost melodies out for a spine
rung cathedrals bombard moths of you. Shopfront wassail. Pollarding.
    Bluster ready masthead rig with this
      silence. In city apparel this silence
        drawing sodium thoroughfare lit vapour making
          a run of you yet irradiate melodies spine out for

fuck chewing to whistle you've anthemic dog a notch in your heart
scarring five other people you made countable. Transact this fuck out
    of another guise love drawn wassailed
      archived. In glib rung virtuoso archive
    transacted love cockring groceries bitingly stop
    saying love which has not been paid for violence now

dogs unwhistling chew. Vuvuzela dribbling shit lesions baton whistling
constituent weals chisel grained wounds over grained up muslin. Over
    provided transient suns down bridleways
      sodden. Full already away sodden
        fat and away nostalgic whinnying autumn eutrophy now
        chiselled out porn adobe visor state farrier silences

fill in filled gaps. Worst tributary back case space complexity
bluster rungs thy tender mercy's sake a moth of you clocks it this
sun's light here shouting riot aplomb
unendurable. Crochet each unendurable
square inch of shard to skin together a horse
in pure sun purely depth first mercy search sun for

leather truly apart from dog water siren. Radiant care perturb
countable *Londons* oil and watering out to unendurable sex
truly ramified bifurcate wholly open
rung. Where constable am I rung
straight mute over brassed water gong sirens dog gong
multiphonics screaming I do not love

you or want to fuck you either until they have paid. There is a cop
pissing into my happiest mouth. Cry for splitting this open
a dog whistle apart from sirens
splitting this open
apart from water
nothing

Song

and can't stop drinking myself entirely out of my favourite
to spring there are more and more birds in my poems, they're
absolutely cherish
                        absolutely threatened not by numbers
or eventual extinction but each tight individually and pressed
from incandescent curfew terror, with snow, with sunburn, the
flame distinctly meet and join men who scream down phones,
cocaine on a banknote that you loved, bells, jutting things seen
could be anything or only metal, it doesn't matter   only
influence over birds is pure and baleful they are frozen
it is mine
and really I do care about them, truly
                            but can't help them, I
am taking out my drinking on them, it is much like being pro-

they are not real birds even, most likely gaps in fog sharp
toward delicacy glints oh air gap in a sky fat with
mechanically de-boned meat full of shit and selling and shaking:

It's true that I don't feel well or know anything about birds   that
and covered in cum and wake exactly where I was and again
and have a drink which actually has nothing to do with birds
these birds are nothing to do with birds
jesus christ we came so much didn't we
grit and dirt in the sky is   pearls closed off to us, I love you
birds are black-hearted pieces of shit unsinging
                            they thrill to be hurt
                            yes your calf muscles
                            the other morning I'd
                            like it was a totally

worlds, so
everywhere. They're

alone thinking with
fucking police, universal anger, dogs that
the amount of
from a distance

foundly lonely shattering at every blistering real moment,
                                        exactly that. Most likely

I want to be fucked
drugs to be fucked and covered

I look at them
matter to me
woken up
normal thing to do but I hadn't and I hate it

(8.ix.2012)

Voicemail for David Hoyle

*written and recorded the night before the fifth show of Illus-
tration, 13ᵗʰ November 2014; the recording was played while
David painted*

david. hi – david, it's me, it's timothy
the line isn't great

i was in the dark watching the foxes playing fox chess and
    wound up
you should see this
maybe out the window past the foxes you actually can see
    this, it's

just the other side of the viaduct, there's
to begin with there
this sparking streetlamp with its wires bared and the
    plastic and
the bulb's ripped out

that artist whose entire life and work i forget
the one who so prized that pink you get in newly lit
    electric lamps
he employed these boys to steal them and grind them down
    for paint

they are back to
murder him in this sinkhole where the water is rising from
    the drains

that artist who disguised violence as whimsy and papered
    over the shattering that fell like teeth in a dream from the
    gaps in lives he hoped he'd be paid to grout

who i never did punch in the face even for being imagined
if he'd been real
you would have spat plague and expensive death into his paint
    with me

there's a fox helping the corner of my eye

but the boys were real and the lamps they ground to dust were
    real and the dust that was never the same colour as the
    lamps was real and it's happening
and it isn't just the one streetlamp or the one boy

that world is growing back through to join the moonlight and
    fling out tendrils of limbs and mouths and heart and skin
    toward it
and naked as kindness they're clawing up the grille of every
    motorway bridge, in all their hinges and sex these boys are
    as fast as paint

the poison water from the drains must be a foot deep by now
and i'm climbing with them, the ground is gone now, my feet
    are soaked through and already rotting

every angle is here, a hundred thousand lost
boys finally stopped grinding brand new lamplight to a failed
    unpink powder
lashing, ardently with ropes of their ripped clothes and hair,
    each other, full of love and anger, to each other, way beyond
    the ringroad
high as a kite off the chevrons on a given roundabout and
    climbing tied to each other further above ground than
    we've ever fought

we've made this cordon as big as the sky of our bodies around
    this city that stinks like a bin that will fucking burn in its sump
circles you thought were bubbles on the surface of the living
    wage are the last you will see of mouths you loved and

everything we ever lived has rammed itself further down our
    throats than a relay of these dilatory screams the size of
    lives attenuable to an oyster point will ever scrape out

if my signal drops it's because i've climbed with them, we're so
    high now
i can in one single inverted yawn of my eyes full of skin and
    sex and fury see the whole city i so slowly streetlamp by
    streetlamp from the other side spent my life seeing in a
    drowning

and this one boy here he's doing
he's doing a painting, it's the last day of august, it's a painting
    of a bed and

None of my previous research into ghosts, fog, dust, head-lands, inaccessible light-sources, defunct mechanisms, finches, maps, foxes, or bodies of water, has been useful in communicating with the cat. Even the 'chirrup' which cats produce on entering a room, which has long been known to be a noise cats make only for the benefit of their human companions, is entirely absent here.

It has been ascertained that dogs bark in order to check whether they are still alive. Even in the case of those barks which we suppose are intended for us, the primary function still operates. Dogs which are ghosts can still bark, but we rarely hear it; perhaps they hear so quickly that they are ghosts that the bark is curtailed immediately, in surprise or fear.

Now, ghosts which are cats, which is to say, defunct cat-mechanisms which are bodies of ghosts subject tidally to the open lake of a raised floor, are an absent chirrup. Sometimes a fabric flattens and do you miss anyone, such as cats. Inaccessibly fog dust. To double-check the ramified map of how alive I am, barked back a fog. Through you a dog is pecked. Chirrup.

Open water between a light source and how dust is become a headland, do you see. Yet how an interim is a fox headland or phrased differently not yet inaccessible is the crucial map: the eyes of ghost cats splinter into a mirrored network, the light source distantly reflected, almost certainly the flicker of ghost water meeting itself along a shear.

Open ghosts flicker to check they are interstitial, the opposite cat mechanism to a body of defunct water unpouring yet and where tidally must the light sources eye by eye be reintroduced. A gull by any other angle of incidence retires the diary into again, is it alive, the flicker of open water meeting a willed unhaunting silently and without feedback: a brief headland become immediately dust, in defunct surprise or inaccessible fear.

ACKNOWLEDGEMENTS

For material included in this selection the following grateful acknowledgements are made: to Penguin Books (USA) for poems by Michael Robbins from *Alien vs. Predator* (2012) and *The Second Sex* (2014); to Patricia Lockwood for her poems from *Balloon Pop Outlaw Black* (Octopus Books, 2012) and *Motherland Fatherland Homelandsexuals* (Penguin Books (USA), 2014; forthcoming, Penguin Books (UK), 2017); and to Timothy Thornton for his poems from *PESTREGIMENT* (Grasp Press, 2008), *Jocund Day* (Mountain Press, 2011), *TRAILS 01/07/2011* (Deterritorial Support Group, 2011), *Working Together for a Safer London* (Barque Press, 2015), *Water and Burning Effects On/Off* (Shit Valley, 2015) and *Broken Slat From Starling* (The Winter Olympics, 2015).

Poems by Michael Robbins first appeared in *Fence*, *Hazlitt*, *HTML Giant*, *Lemon Hound*, *The New Yorker*, *Poetry* and *Prelude*; by Patricia Lockwood, in *The Awl*, *Colorado Review*, *Hayden's Ferry Review*, *London Review of Books*, *Poetry*, *Rattle*, *The Seattle Review* and *Slate*; and by Timothy Thornton, in *Better Than Language: An Anthology of New Modernist Poetries* (Ganzfeld, 2011), *Cambridge Literary Review*, *Deterritorial Support Group*, *Hi Zero* and *Poems, Written Between October and December 2010* (Grasp Press, 2011, with Jonny Liron, Francesca Lisette and Joseph Luna).